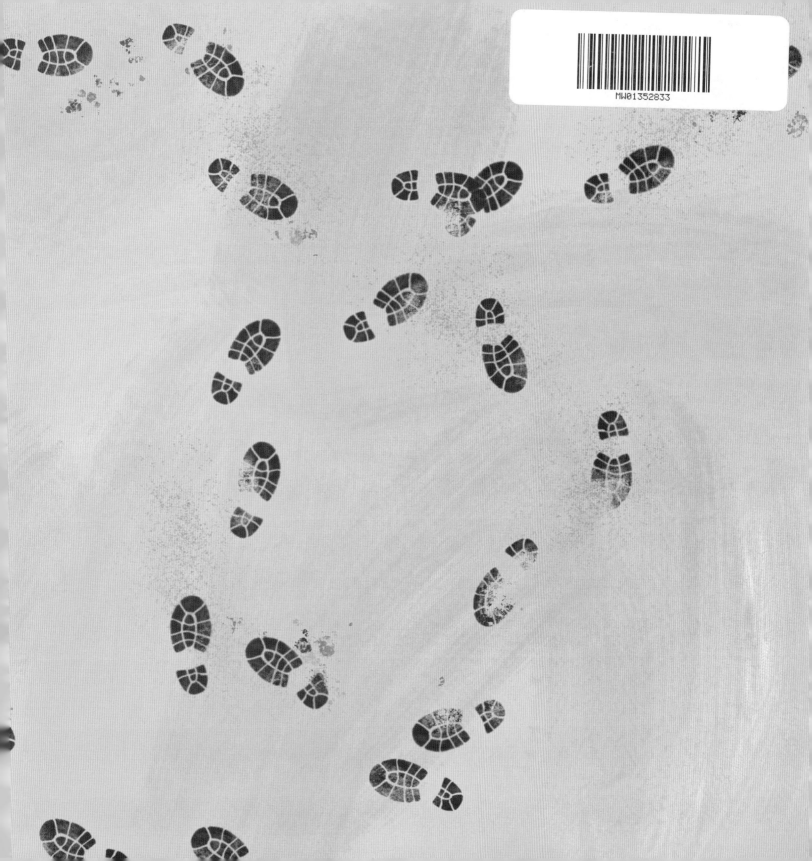

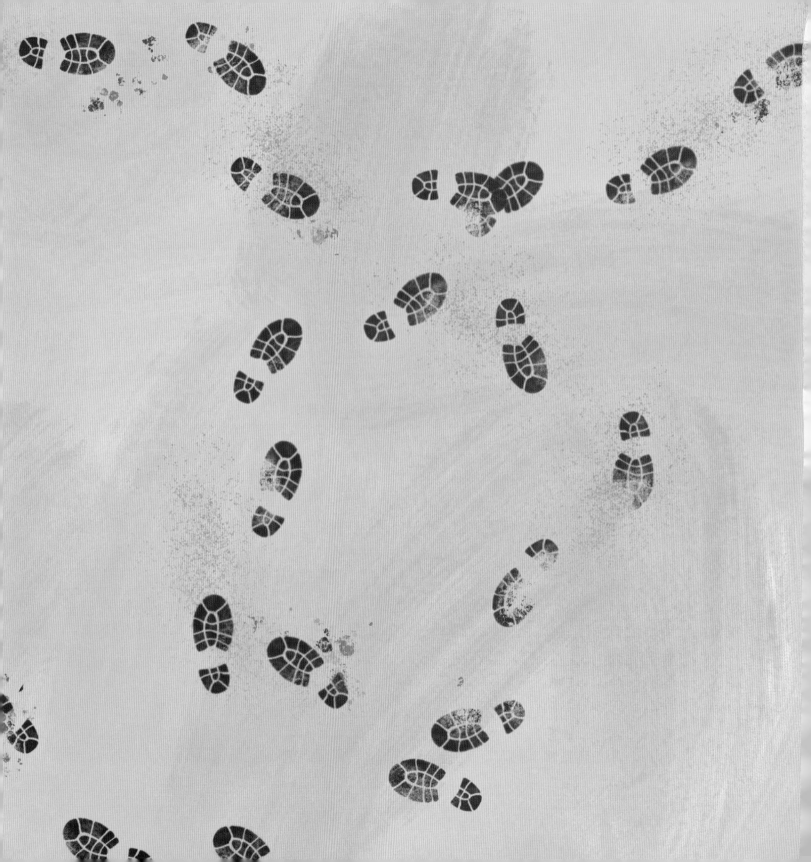

Nature Parade

For Cooper and Grace, may you always find joy in the little things. —N. S.

For all nature spirits and mushroom hunters, and especially for my family. —M. H.

Text copyright © 2021 by Nikki Samuels
Illustrations copyright © 2021 by Martina Heiduczek
Book design by David Miles

All Rights Reserved. No part of this publication may be reproduced, stored in a retrieval system, or transmitted, in any form or by any means, electronic, mechanical, photocopying, recording, or otherwise, without prior written permission from the publisher.

First Edition 2021
Printed and bound in China
Library of Congress Control Number 2020925920

ISBN 978-1-7364030-1-3

Tiny Twigs Press, LLC
www.tinytwigspress.com

Nature Parade

Nikki Samuels

Illustrations by
Martina Heiduczek

Out in the woods, two red shoes come to play,
dusty and worn, perfect pair for the day.

They hop, skip, and run, climbing high as they go,
"Hello!" the shoes call as the sun shines below.
Further ahead, the shoes hear a song,
faintly at first, till others join along.

Whirling and twirling, the wind starts to blow,

Whoosh, whoosh, whoosh!

Dancing fast and then slow.

The leaves are the next to pick up the beat,

Crunch, crunch, crunch!

Chasing after the feet.

Feeling the rhythm, a rock starts to roll,

Thump, thump, thump!

Bouncing over a hole.

A bird sings its song from up in the trees,

Chirp, chirp, chirp!

Adding notes to the breeze.

A grasshopper sways to nature's sweet tune,

Snap,

snap,

snap!

Jumping high as the moon.

The shoes take a rest, looking up as they pause.
A new sound is here and the clouds are the cause.

Droplets of rain start to fall from the sky,

Plop, plop, plop!

Filling puddles up high.

Splashing and stomping, the shoes join the fun!

Splish, splish, splish!

Tossing mud as they run.

It's a nature parade! With the sounds they've all made.

Whoosh!

Crunch!

Thump! *Chirp!*

Buzz!

Snap! *Plop!*

Splish!

This marvelous tune travels up and around,
filling the woods with magnificent sound.

"Yippee! Wahoo! Hooray!"

Cheer the shoes as they play.

The music plays on until dusk, when it slows. The shoes take a bow and then shout, "Time to go!"

The raindrops let up while the grasshopper rests,
the bee becomes still and the bird finds its nest.
The rock nestles into the mud on the ground,
while the leaves settle down without making a sound.

All is now quiet, the wind just a whisper.
The sun has sunk down and the air's a bit crisper.

Speckled with dirt on their laces and soles, turning towards home, their pace now a stroll.

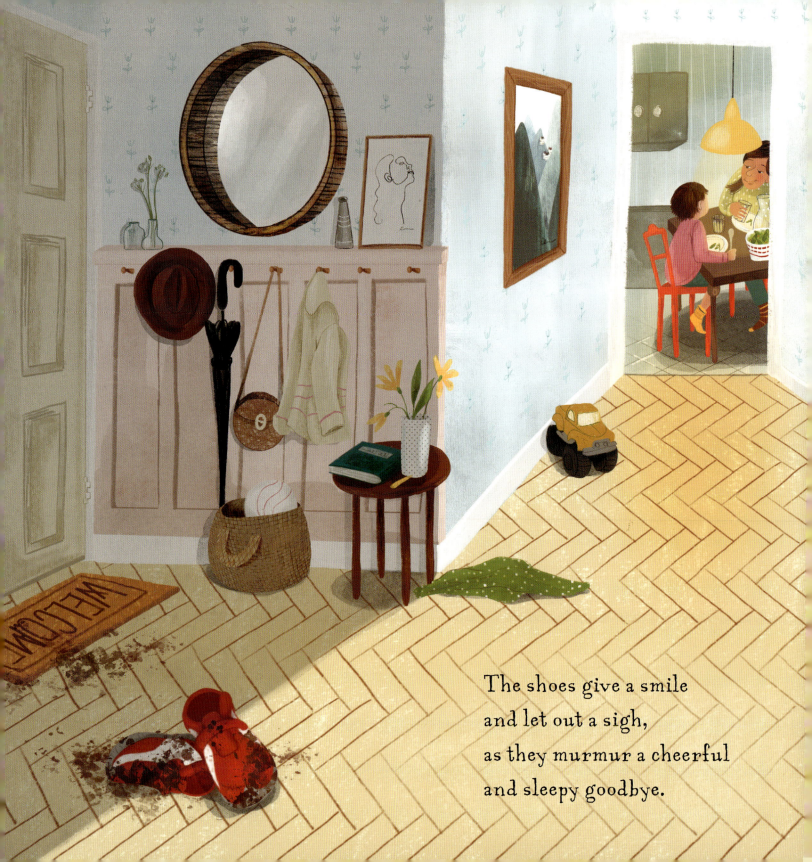

The shoes give a smile
and let out a sigh,
as they murmur a cheerful
and sleepy goodbye.

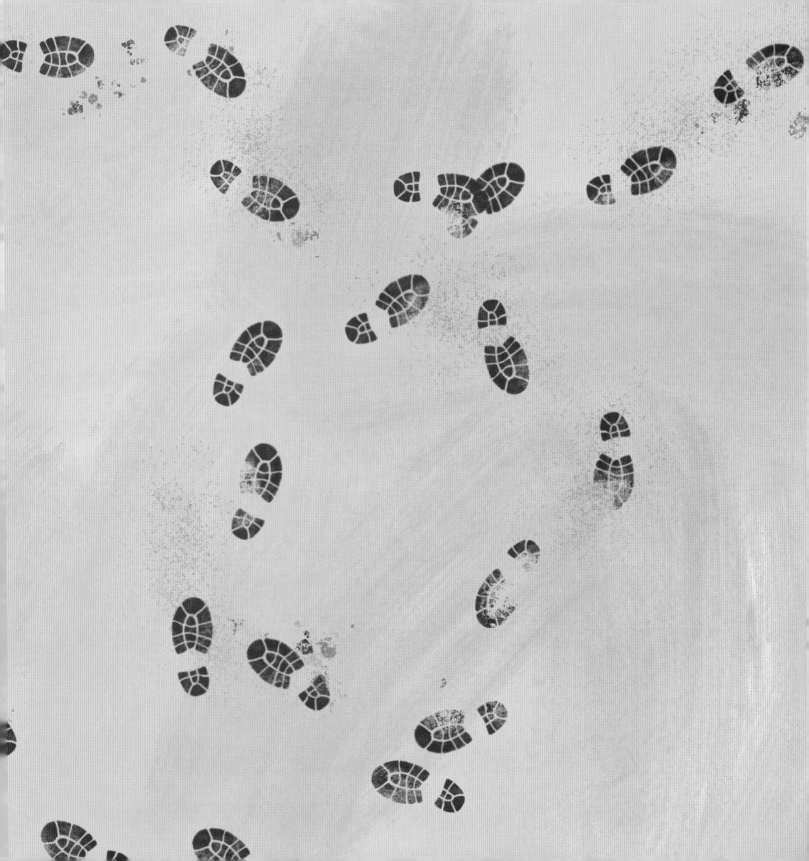

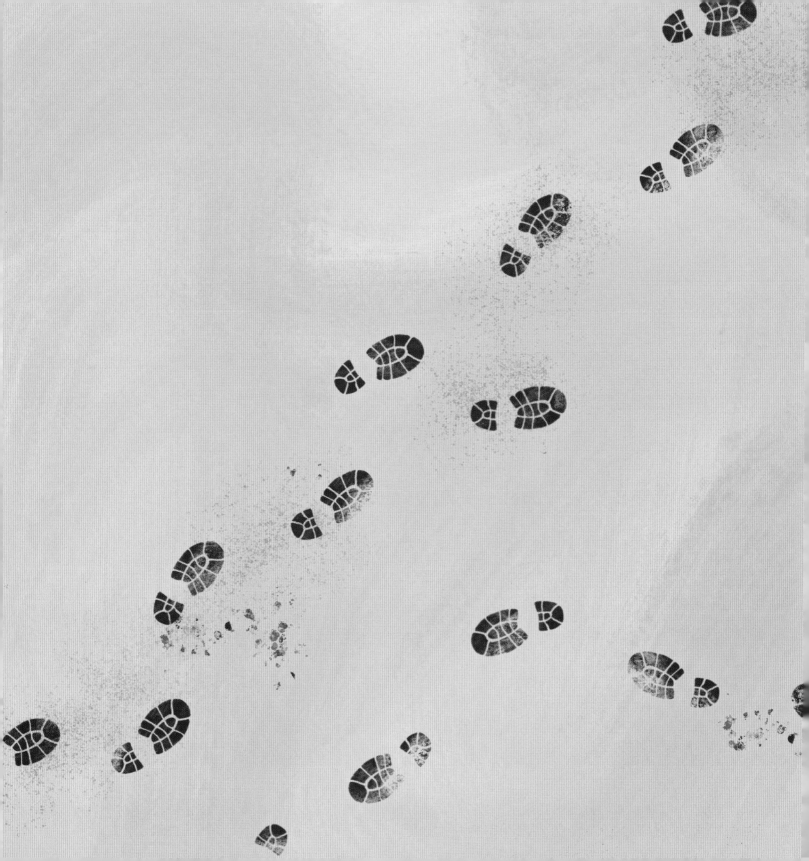